Will You Be M...
Based On A True Story
Through The Eyes And Ears Of Autism

Written By
Grant Harrison

Illustrated By
Katrin Xalti

Copyright © April 2022
By Grant Harrison & Tracy Bruce-Harrison

All rights reserved. No part of this book or its characters may be reproduced in any manner without written permission, unless in the case of quotations embedded into brief positive articles or reviews.

ISBN#9798444562604

www.fetchtheswell.com
@fetchtheswell
@exploring_together_autism

Dedications

To my mom, dad, and brother you are the most amazing family ever. I would not be who I am today without all your love, support, and guidance But for mainly telling and showing me how special I am. I love you so much.

To Samantha, I dedicate this book to you and other kids who are nonverbal. I am just honored to be your voice for Autism and to be your cousin. You are an inspiration to all of us.

To Grandma, you are amazing in so many ways. Thank you for always being and looking out for all of us. I love you

Grant sat quietly at the kitchen table just staring into his bowl of cereal. "Hey buddy, why such the long face this morning?" Mom asked, as she slowly lifted his head up to only see the tears building up in his eyes.

"Mom, I don't want to go to school today. Our teacher said we are going to do a group project." "So, what's so terrible about that?" his mom asked.

Grant put his head down again and said, "No one ever chooses me. I fidget so much in class. I think it scares them off."

Grant's mom put his hands in hers and said, "Look at me, Grant." He did and she said, "You are a very special person, and you need to always remember that." She continued, "Remember son, there is nothing we can't handle together. You are never alone." He smiled at her and said, "I love you, Mom."

Mrs. Klida, Grant's teacher, came into the room and said, "Good morning class! I was just informed our school is going to have a talent show. Nothing would excite me more than to see each of you sign up! You can work in groups if that makes it easier." Everyone immediately started picking their groups, but once again, Grant was alone.

 Mrs. Klida saw this and immediately walked over to Grant, leading another student, and said, "Hey Grant, this is Jessica. She is new to our class. I think you two will work well together."

 Grant was too nervous to respond. He thought, "What if she doesn't want to work with me?"

 Jessica spoke up and said, "I would love to work with you, Grant. I'm super excited!"

Later, when Grant entered the lunchroom, he noticed the new student was sitting at the lunch table by herself. He noticed because this usually happened to him.

"Can I sit here?" Grant asked. "Sure! That would be great!" Jessica replied. Then, to his surprise, he saw her pull something round out of her pocket. "What's that?" he asked. Jessica smiled and said, "It's a worry rock. I have a lot of anxiety and fidget all the time, so this helps me keep my hands busy so it's not so noticeable in class."

"Wow!" Grant thought to himself. "Maybe I'm not so different from other people after all." From that moment on, he and Jessica started working out what they would do for the talent show, laughing and enjoying their time together.

 As usual, Grant's mom was waiting for him at the bus stop. "Mom, I made a friend today and we're going to be in the school talent show together!" he shouted as he exited the bus. Grant's mom smiled and let out a heartfelt sigh of relief to finally see Grant so excited.

Over the next couple of weeks, Grant and his new friend worked together in class to get their talent show act ready.

"Mom, can you help me set up my equipment for the talent show?" Grant asked. His mom replied, "No worries, Son. I will have it all ready for you at the school."

Just before the show started, Grant asked, "Jessica do you have your worry stone with you?" Thinking she might be as nervous as him. "Actually Grant, I brought two with me and I want you to have one." She handed Grant one that read, "My friend." Grant felt so happy because that was the moment he knew he found an amazing, life-long friend.

Jessica stood at the podium and did a wonderful introduction for Grant. Then, the curtains opened. Students had filled the auditorium. They were in awe when they saw Grant—the kid without friends who fidgets all the time—sitting behind a shiny new drum set.

Then, the music began, and Grant played his heart out. When the music ended, all the kids were cheering and yelling his name. He felt like a superstar.

When the talent show was over, and it was time to go back to class, Grant and Jessica took their time walking back together. Grant pulled the worry stone from his pocket Jessica gave him and said, "Thank you. I couldn't have done it without you and this worry rock." Jessica blushed and said, "No, thank you, Grant, for being my friend."

 They entered the classroom and to Grant's surprise, his teacher and all the kids were all standing, clapping, and cheering their names. Grant shed tears of joy because this was the first time he felt like people finally saw him as someone more than just the kid who fidgets. All while standing next to his new best friend.

A Special Thank You!!
Resources For Autism

Thank you for all your support, patience, and guidance I would not have been able to complete my book without you.

Katrin Xalti
@katrin_Xalti
My Amazing Freelance illustrator

Terry Maley - My Aunt and Biggest Advocator
Speech, Occupational Therapy
www.sammyssensorystuff
www.developingconnections.com

Christy McFarland
@Christychrisbooks
Children's Book - Narwin The Narwhal

Lynne Greaves
Amazing Work Books For Children
@emotions_learning_content
https://emotionslearningco.wixsite.com/books

Nine Tails Comics
@ninetailscomics
Kids Math Educational Comics

Grant Harrison

Friends Autograph

Friends Autograph

Made in the USA
Middletown, DE
12 July 2022